Freedom Café Farewell Cookbook

W/Mississippi Addendum

Janice & James Swinton

DEDICATION

This book is dedicated to our spiritual daughter, Amanda Kelly, who worked tirelessly for us and has been a faithful and true spiritual daughter; may God continue to grow you in His stature and help you reach your amazing destiny in Him.

Table of Contents

Farewell!!

As we have announced our retirement many customers have asked me what we plan to do in Mississippi, and if we plan on opening another café. My first answer is I don't know what we will be doing in Mississippi, only God has that answer, just as when I moved to Maine I didn't have a clue what we would be doing. It's up to God. My second response is "NO"; I absolutely have no plans of opening another restaurant.

This time I want to really be able to focus on ministry and writing. I realized that even though I thought I wanted to be a hermit and live in the woods and write when I moved to Maine, I wasn't ready to "live in the woods" and God knew that. I also wasn't ready to write because there were many things that I needed to learn and many areas in my life that needed maturing; and God managed to squeeze quite a bit in these 14 years of living in Maine.

So I tell them, "I'm leaving much better than I came." Of course, I have some battle marks and scars, but if you are living life, there will be battles. It is always good to end your journey being able to say "it's been a good run, I've learned many things and I'm not the same woman who crossed over into Maine in 1996."

James and I want to thank all of our faithful customers, workers, friends and enemies, because it has all been more than worth it and we both leave better souls than we came.   This leg of the journey has prepared us for the next leg, and as one road ends and another begins, it is God alone who knows the "end from the beginning," our job is to obey and get going; as is in all of our lives if we pay attention.

Each weekend since we announced our retirement we have heard from our many loyal customers.   Many are sad that we are leaving but encourage us onto the next road.

It has been overwhelming to realize how much community we have shared over the years with many of you; so many that we can't mention you all, but thank you for your patronage and thank you for accepting us and adding us to your extended family and stopping by every now and then for a family meal.   James and I will be forever thankful for our experience here in Maine.

Chapter One:

Higher Ground:
How we got to 144 College Avenue!

Flooding called 'act of God'

WATERVILLE- The Easter Sunday flooding
caused by a broken water main on Silver
Street was called an "act of God" Wednesday
by the general manager of the Kennebec Water
District. (Morning Sentinel, Thursday, April 12, 2007)

Transitions can be very messy, and we found the transition from 18 Silver Street to our present location quite messy. For me, transitions always seem to start with trouble. Not unlike women giving birth, the water breaks, and it signals a transition. In the fall of 2006, it was also "water" that signaled the transition to 144 College Avenue.

In November of 2006 it was a very rainy season. Down on 18 Silver Street in the basement the water was seeping into the carpets and eventually we had to use a wet vacuum to suck it up. It was the same week that my first cookbook had arrived in boxes from the publisher in Lenexa, Kansas. I couldn't get excited about the book because on Tuesday

7

morning, my dessert chef went to work at the café, opened the door, and a flood of water came rushing out the back door. The café, over the weekend, had flooded. There was about a foot of water in the lower half of the café. We were shocked. The insurance didn't pay for the cleanup because it happened from the inside of the building. Of course, we had no flood insurance and had to pay for the cost of cleanup from already strained funds. It rocked our comfort zone and made us realize that this was a sign from God to James and me, that it was time to move to higher ground.

In addition, my health had been compromised too many times at Silver Street because the capacity was twice that of this new place. I knew that I could not keep up that pace and remain healthy, so this in addition to the flood, made us seek God for direction.

He directed us here to 144 College Avenue. The transition was hard because we still had to pay rent at Silver Street for ten months after we bought this place. In fact, it was financially draining to transition. But I knew that it was God's way of getting us out of that situation and positioning us to move.

It became quite clear that it was the hand of God moving and directing us when that Easter 2007, the water pipe broke on Silver Street sending 2.5 million gallons of water rushing into businesses and basements downtown. The basement flooded and it caused a lot of damage to businesses and especially the ones in the basements. Our café had been located in the basement and we would have been "out of business" with no flood insurance and no way to recover.

So, like Noah, God sent the first flood to let us know we needed to move to higher ground before the big flood came that would have closed our business. Although the transitions were messy and financially draining, remaining in the basement at Silver Street would have ultimately cost us everything; we would not have been able to recoup.

In the realm of God things happen first in the natural realm and then in the spiritual. If you are experiencing a lot of trouble in the natural realm, check your spiritual life and see what's happening.

The moral to this story is pay attention to the God signs; if things are getting uncomfortable where you are, it might be time to move to higher ground.

Freedom Cafe:
Starting with the Ending

Writing this cookbook turned out to be more emotional than I had anticipated. Like most journeys in life when you come to the end of one road, and look toward the next road in front of you, it becomes clear that what was will no longer be and all the good, bad, and ugly on the road you are leaving has formed you into a new and different version of yourself, one that you didn't want or desire, but the one that God knew you needed to become. That would define the ending of my journey here at the café. When I crossed over that Maine line in 1996 I didn't know what was ahead of me on that road. I was a much wounded woman and really just wanted to go sit by the sea and cry out to Jesus to heal me. I didn't want to be around people or even involved with them. I had received wounds from many before leaving Lawrence, Kansas, and really just wanted to lick my wounds, hide out and heal.

But I knew the person that I had become because of these traumas wasn't the one that God wanted me to stay. You see, life changes us; it changes us into better or worse souls. I didn't want to be where I had come to be so I cried out for God to heal me and He did. After all, the wounds that I had received had come on the battle line serving Him. I was His soldier and I had been wounded by arrows from my fellow soldiers, "friendly fire", or so they looked like His soldiers but most were not.

It didn't take me long to understand that the school of learning and the lessons had only begun. Ahead of me has been this amazing journey, again with the good, bad, and ugly that has again formed me, but praise to my God – this time, He didn't allow me to go down. When I would fall down, He picked me backup and pushed me forward. When I thought I wanted to leave and run away, He wouldn't let me; when people who were supposed to be friends turned into deceivers and liars, He taught me how to forgive their offenses and let go of those toxic emotions; toxic emotions that would physically and spiritually kill me before them. I learned how to change how I thought therefore changing how I live and see the world around me.

I learned what a broken heart feels like, and how disappointment after disappointment can make the heart sick but formed in me not to expect what I want in people because that wasn't going to happen. I learned that I can't carry people, no matter how much I love them and want to help them, because I simply breakdown, and drop them; and then Jesus has to rescue us both.

I have learned that there really are evil men in the world who will cheat you and take your money; I learned that people will and do lie, without batting an eyelid.

I learned that family isn't always biological and that people will help you and look out for your interest. Which brings me to this very important THANK YOU to all of my family of employees that have hung in there with James and I; thanks to Bonnie Bissonette; Mike and Lori Dumont, Nick, Michael and Emily; Lisa Gurney and her son Ben; Darlene Dostie another kitchen partner; my spiritual daughter and dessert chef Amanda Kelly; to another spiritual daughter, Heidi Rioux, waitress; Michelle' Mendez; Robert and Ann Foshay and their sons, Tim, Michael and Ethan; Kristen and Lauren Brooks, Michele and Daniel Rossignol, Alasdair, Peter, Frank, Kevin, and Chris; and many more.

As I finally began putting recipes to paper it was a very emotional feeling of the labor of love of the past eleven years and the many people that we have fed and comforted with plates of warm, loved filled, vibration cooking. As I write, it is an ending and a beginning at the same time. It signals I am ending this end of the journey here in Waterville, Maine, and that leaving will not be easy, but the season has ended and it's is time to move on. Returning to my southern roots seems more poignant after having learned and served part of that history here in the North. I learned more about cooking and serving soul food here in Maine than in the south. And I learned more about being a southerner living here in the north.

As a gift to my loyal patrons here are my farewell recipes that you have enjoyed over these past years. The next couple of chapters are the last chapters from my first cook book, included to bring customers up to date who aren't familiar with our history and how we got started. The rest is new, bringing you up-to-date with the journey here and a host of favorite recipes never before printed but often requested. God bless!

Introduction

I was eight when my father became ill and was bedridden. It was at this tender age I began a cycle of using food as a comforter to inner turmoil and emotional hurts, as well as happy times. I didn't fully understand it at that time but later in life the pattern would repeat itself -- over and over again. I would eat half gallons of Borden's Lemon Custard ice cream while hiding underneath the back porch. I devoured five-pound bags of M&Ms, boxes of Baby Ruth's and Snicker bars there in my hiding place. This was my way of dealing with my father's sudden illness. I was a daddy's girl and he had been my hero. I remember sitting on the front steps as a preschooler waiting for my father to walk from the alley across the street from where he worked at the chemical plant. As soon as I saw him I raced across the street and down the gravel alley to jump into his arms. I was daddy's little girl and he always had a treat for me. He always saved me a piece of candy or half a sandwich from his lunch. When he became ill I was too young and emotionally immature to deal with seeing my hero become a helpless invalid. I ate to comfort myself but later I would learn to cook and feed my father to comfort him as well.

When I was around the age of fifteen, mom began to allow me to take turns "daddy-sitting" while she took the family to church on Saturdays. By this time daddy had been an invalid for seven years. Whenever it was my turn to stay home alone with daddy I immediately went into the kitchen, baked homemade oatmeal cookies, fried fish, French fries, and fed my father. It was my way of comforting him and me. I also enjoyed watching him eat my cooking. It was our time together. He sat in his wheelchair on the front porch, while I held the plate of food for him as he ate with his one good hand, "Want some more Daddy; I'd ask? He would always shake his head, 'yes,' for more and off to the kitchen I went mixing flour, sugar, butter, oatmeal, vanilla, and salt making the cookies he liked best; or breading the fish with cornmeal and salt and pepper to fry it in the cast iron skillet. It was here that I began to learn that food could be a means of comforting others or comforting oneself.

Farewell Addendum: *As I leave I read these words and realize that I too have shared my love for comfort food with literally thousands of people right here in Maine and from all over the world. My love for comfort and to comfort others filled many plates here at the café; if it was just a bad day at work or the death of a loved one we* *have been there; if it was just a "girl's night out" we were here; birthdays, graduations, wedding rehearsals, and everything in between — we have been here to comfort you with good food and good company. Janice*

Chapter Two:
Freedom Cafe:

Leap of Faith

Before moving to Maine, while living in Lawrence, Kansas, I had often entertained the idea of opening my own restaurant or coffee shop. I'm not real sure where the desire came from but a seed had somehow been planted. My idea in Lawrence was for an upscale southern restaurant named "The Delta." I had visions of decor with Magnolia flowers and lots of antiques. What I didn't have a vision for was the cuisine. I gave little thought to what I would cook, just the place.

The idea somehow got lost in the muddle of everyday life and its usual challenges and stresses. After moving to Maine, I worked in Portland and gave no thoughts to a restaurant but the theme of "freedom from the rat race" was never far from my mind: Freedom to serve God, and freedom of choice in how I spent my days, working for myself instead of under someone else; the freedom to change the course of my life and not to fear taking risks. The idea of a juice bar resurfaced upon our return to Kansas City to attend Jim's mother's funeral in March of 1998. After the funeral, we visited friends in Lawrence and stopped into a juice bar downtown. For the first time I had a shot of wheat grass and a delicious smoothie. Death in the family always has a way of causing you to take a look at the dreams that you keep putting off; because death makes you realize that you might not have long.

Upon our return to Maine the stirring to simplify our lives caused us to begin looking at the idea of a coffee shop and juice bar again. My prayer was show me how to simplify my life, live freer so I could seek Him. The notion that life was not meant to be lived the way that I was living it was ever-present in my mind. This time James and I began writing down what we would need to begin such an endeavor. Our lists covered equipment, space, parking, and juice extractors.

I began experimenting with health conscious breads, muffins, and cookies that I could make and sell. I grew some wheat grass and used several of the juice extractors I had purchased at Marden's. I began making fruit smoothies again, experimenting with different flavors. Because we were vegetarians at that time I created delicious turkey burgers and veggie burgers to be sold. My homemade whole-wheat bread was to die for.

For the next several months, we would discuss our plans with no definite starting point because we had absolutely no money. The fact that we had no experience starting a business never dawned on us either. We spent a lot of time praying, seeking God's direction and wisdom, because we didn't dare step out and risk so much if He wasn't directing our steps. Each prayer felt more and more like a "yes." We were heading in the right direction.

By the summer of 1998, we had looked at a few properties; researched purchasing books for the bookstore, still financially broke. The idea was to save enough money to get started but that was impossible. There wasn't enough there to put aside any great amounts so by the time September rolled around there was only $900.00 in our savings account. The difference was I was desperate to run for my life. I felt I needed to get out of that hospital in order to live because the situation had worsened and going to work was hard.

That September, after hiking Mohegan Island with friends from Kansas, I had another outbreak from the sun with severe swelling and blistering of my face and arms. This time it was bad enough that they put me on prednisone and my primary physician sent me to a specialist to be tested for possible

19

lupus. This was the third outbreak since summer and I felt it represented the need for change - Now!

While fully blistered and burnt, I went to downtown Waterville to pick up my prescription on a Saturday morning. As was the habit I went to a couple of my favorite shops, one was The Picket Fence. There I found a set of colorful dinnerware and platters that I put on lay-a-way, thinking they would look wonderful in the coffee shop, which I did not have yet. In fact, I had made quite a few purchases for this future shop, including the juice extractors. As I left downtown, on the Spring Street connector I saw a "For Rent' sign in one the buildings behind Silver Street. I drove down, peeped into the window, and saw the brick walls. It seemed the perfect place. I wrote down the phone number and drove home to tell Jimmy about it. I called the owner who was willing to show us the place, in short order. Apparently, the space had been a coffee shop that lasted less than a year.

I warned Jimmy before we left the house to see the place, and not to say anything about us being broke. He is the conservative and logical one in our marriage. I am the impulsive, spontaneous, "everything will work out" kind of girl.

The space had a lot of things that we had included on our list. It was much larger than what I thought I needed but it had the brick walls, the ceiling that was unfinished showing all the wires, wooden beams, and pipes. The rustic unfinished look of the place was perfect for a quaint, cozy coffee shop.

I know I didn't impress the owners with my high enthusiasm without concrete plans for the space. When asked, "What do you want to do?"

My response was completely random, "I'm not sure. It maybe a coffee shop with a few sandwiches, a juice bar, entertainment and plays, a gathering place, or a hermitage. I really don't know yet."

James was quietly in the background looking and thinking like the wise owl that he is, but he kept quiet about the lack of funds.

The owner told me that someone else had looked at it earlier, thinking about doing an "internet cafe." I asked him what the rent was, he told me the amount and that I would need to put $500.00 down in order to secure it. I said, "Okay."

The only thing I felt confident about was that when we walked into the place and began looking around and praying, God was saying, "This is the place, trust Me." Since I've always believed that God orders my steps, I had to believe Him now in this risky venture. A few weeks later, we signed a four-year lease and began the unknown journey into the food service business. Little did we know?

James, who had been unable to find any permanent job since moving to the Waterville area, jumped right into fixing up and getting things up to code. The previous tenant had done quite a bit of work considering when he rented the basement it was just that, a brick basement. He and his partner cleaned and blasted the brick walls, installed steps and doors, and installed a heating system with an exhaustion system as well. They also built a bathroom and installed sinks, electrical outlets, counter-tops, and shelving. Basically they took a basement and brought it up to code for a coffee shop. It cost them thousands of dollars to get all of this done.

It was as though God had ordained this place for us because there was no way we could have ever afforded to fix it up. Not only did we not have thousands of dollars; we only had $400 left.

The first expense came in the form of getting utilities turned on so James could get to work. My lack of business knowledge was put to the test when I was told I needed to deposit $1000 dollars to get the electricity turned on. I was shocked, which the CMP lady on the other end felt. She tried to explain to me that the deposit amount was based on the previous tenant's usage. They took the highest monthly bills and came up with that amount. I explained that there was no way I could come up with that amount and wouldn't be open seven days a week as the previous tenant. She was therefore able to reduce the amount to $600 and arranged it so I could pay it in 3 monthly installments. It was tight, but we got the electricity turned on. The water and phone were reasonable.

The fact remained that we could not afford high rent plus utilities on the cafe and the house we were renting. Immediately, we began looking to find a cheaper apartment to rent. At the time, we had a large three-bedroom house on Johnson Avenue and paid over $700 for rent and utilities. There was no way we could afford the $600+ that we needed to pay for the cafe as well. I saw an advertisement for a small apartment in a professional building on Silver Street. I called and found out it belonged to one of the physicians I knew at the hospital. There were two other apartments in the building and the first floor was used for the doctor's practice. The price was right, $275 a month, so we moved up to the third floor apartment.

This meant that we had to move all of our furniture, artwork, pictures, dining room furniture, and sofas down to the cafe. These gave the cafe that homey feeling. The largest piece of furniture we moved to the new apartment was our bed. It wasn't ideally what I wanted but we needed to sacrifice in order to get the restaurant going. It was quiet and peaceful with good tenants and a good landlord.

The next step was repurchasing the grease trap from the Augusta used restaurant equipment place for $275. We went back later to purchase the required three-bay sink. With each paycheck we paid our household bills and took the rest to pay the rent for the restaurant bills, which included the rent and utilities. What was left we used to purchase things for the cafe.

Money was very tight and my job was the only source of income, while James worked on the cafe. Most of the time we were simply broke. The table and chairs were put on lay-away until we got them paid off. We purchased used refrigerators and the landlord let us use an old electric stove he had in storage. The one thing that was previous left in the cafe was a Vulcan pizza oven that belonged to Bruce;

he gave it to us to use as well. Most of our dishes came from Marden's and all the decorations in the café came from our house to enhance the homey feeling.

For months, Jimmy worked at the cafe fixing things, painting, and repairing. I went to work at the hospital and came down in the evening, if I had the energy, to see how things were progressing and to try to visualize the end product. This was our routine from October 1998 until we opened in May of 1999. That winter we went through the correct channels at City Hall to secure a victualer license, then through the Health Department to get inspected and get clearance to open! With all this in place, we still were clueless about what would happen or even how to run and manage a restaurant!

James and I had several opening dates: one in February, then in March and April. Truly we never felt we were ready to open. "Ready" meant you knew what you were doing and we didn't have that confidence. Finally, in May, events beyond our control forced us into opening. The local newspaper came to interview us and we had to give them an opening date, so it became May 25, 1999. Once the newspaper ran the article, opening day was upon us! I had no idea what to cook and had not prepared anything beforehand. I went to work that day and worried about the night at hand. I left work early, drove to the local Shop-n-Save, and purchased some chicken, collard greens, red beans and cans of peaches. Then I ran down to prepare the food before we had to swing open the doors of "Freedom Cafe" for the first time. The red beans were still cooking and the cornbread was still in the oven when people began arriving that evening. James and I had absolutely no plan, no prices, no anything; we basically gave away the food to the fifty or so guests that came through the doors that first night! It was considered a success!

Chapter Three: Freedom Café in the Making

On The Job Training

What to do next? The doors were now officially open and neither of us had a clue. I was still working as a manager at the hospital, which meant my time was divided. I really wanted to jump into this new venture but knew we needed capital to fund it, which at this time, was my paycheck. If I quit too early there would be no steady money to pay bills at home or at the cafe and it would mean no insurance. We had no savings! If we were wrong, we were busted. If it was God, He would provide. James was cautiously optimistic. My faith was strong and I believed God was ordering our steps - my problem was I was clueless about how to make it work. Up to this point, the only people that I cooked for were my husband and family and now I was attempting to cook for the public.

There were three things that God showed us before we opened the door. First, it was clear that this was a God idea and not a Janice and James' idea, which meant it would not be business as usual. It was to be a gathering place for the community with an atmosphere of peace, fellowship, and good food. Second, we were to open only three days a week - Thursday, Friday and Saturday. Mainly, because James was the chief bottle-washer and I was the only Chef.   In addition to these labor restrictions was the fact that I was still working full-time at the hospital. Being open only three days a week would enable me to continue to work during the day and prepare food for those three nights and lunch on Saturday. The truth be told, there was no way for me to prepare food five or six days a week and still work full-time.

Later, I realized how much wiser God is than us, because these nights are when customers usually went out for dinner.

Third, we were to have a prix-fixed menu or an all inclusive menu - with entree, starch, vegetable, cornbread, dessert, and beverage for one price. This idea came from my childhood and adult experiences. At home, mom always had dessert with dinner, even if it was just a jar of homemade pear preserves or peaches. I loved having something sweet at the end of my meal. In fact, I looked forward to it with great anticipation. The other experience was eating in restaurants and paying one price for the salad, another for the entree, another for the drink, and, boy, if you ordered dessert you had no clue of what the final bill would be. For customers, it is a worry-free dining experience – they know before they order how much their meal will cost so they don't have to worry about a la carte prices - and their meal will be complete from beginning to end.

The problem with this idea was since I had no idea of how to run a restaurant and I didn't know how much food would cost or how to price it accordingly. In the beginning, customers could literally order as much food as would fit on their plates for $8.95. This turned out to be good for advertising the restaurant, because once people heard how much food they received and how good the food was, they eventually began trickling in. I, basically, gave away food the first couple of years in business.

When I first opened I cooked four entrees: Pineapple Jerk Chicken, BBQ beef boneless short ribs, Jambalaya and Mommas Lasagna. These entrees were served with macaroni and cheese, black-eyed peas, collard greens, candied yams, and cornbread of course.

I would purchase food from the local grocers paying retail prices, because I had not learned about vendors. When I did, my food order was too small to purchase from them because of their minimal order amount. I purchased the food, loaded it into my car, and brought it to the cafe to prepare. I had one refrigerator, one pizza oven, and a borrowed electric stove that had only two burners that worked.

James and I had absolutely no money for backup or emergencies. This venture had not been capitalized nor had we taken out any loans. That was the fourth thing we felt led of God not to do; to not borrow money and go into debt. Each night, from whatever we earned, I purchased food in hopes of selling it the next night.

That first summer, we averaged between six to twenty customers per night. This meant James and I could get to know customers and be more social. Often we sat down at their tables, struck up conversations, and sparked friendships. This was good "PR" for business, as most people had no clue about who we were. The problem was because the numbers were not consistent I had to guess how many customers would come each night. I tried to prepare enough food in advance, again because I was the only cook. In the beginning, I often guessed wrong and I had to throwaway a lot of food at the end of the night. As word-of-mouth brought in more customers, the opposite occurred – I would run out of food, unfortunately, early in the evening - 6:30 or so. The customers got smart and began lining up outside the door so when we opened at 5 o'clock, there would be a steady stream of customers coming down the stairs - and we would be full in five minutes. They came early so they could get food before I ran out!

It became increasingly evident that I would have to make the break from Maine General soon. After the transcription mutiny, I had waited to resign until September. During the end of August, business at the cafe began to pick up from some wedding rehearsal dinners and word of mouth.

One of the crucial connections made that August was with Ron H., the Resident Hall Director at Colby College. He asked if I could host his incoming resident hall students here for dinner and their meeting. I said, "Yes" even though I had not really fed that many at once before.

I did the dinner and they have been returning to the cafe every year since then. These students introduced the café to other students and we began to see business from the Colby students. It was also the end of the summer and Maine residents were settling in from camps and getting ready for the winter. Since we had opened the first of June all of the students were gone and summers in Maine mean locals are going to their camps and enjoying the great outdoors. By September, both locals and students began finding us. Thank God for free advertising, as we didn't have money to advertise. That November, Lynn A., a writer for the Kennebec Journal wrote a "Thanksgiving with Soul" article with recipes and the story of the cafe. It was a full page and a half, four-color article with pictures of food, the cafe, and James and I. It was more than we could have ever paid for at that time and it really gave us a huge boost in business. It was definitely a God-send as we served Thanksgiving Dinner that year and the paper advertised the menu, recipes, and the time. We had a good turnout, as a result, and finally Freedom Cafe was out to the public.

This meant I needed to finally leave Maine General and focus my energy on the cafe. By this time my interests were divided and I knew I couldn't do a good job remaining at the hospital. I finally resigned in November and really took the leap of faith. It was also evident that I needed to begin to hire some real help fast. My first attempt at finding help was placing an ad in the paper. The results were not good. The help didn't last. Finally, I prayed and asked God to send the people that He wanted to work with me and He did and continued to, periodically cleaning house when necessary.

It didn't help that I had major trust issues resulting from the problems of personnel and personalities that I had just come through at Maine General. I wasn't in a hurry to allow anyone to get close to me and had put up a fresh wall to make sure of it. I was still bleeding from my wounds and still felt the knives in my back.

For almost six months starting in May of 1999, I singlehandedly prepared all the food at the cafe. The service needed lots of help and people waited patiently while the wait-people took their orders, came back behind the counter, fixed the plates, and then took the plates out to the table. What a zoo! In addition to this chaos, the people I had working for me were inexperienced, immature teenagers. And because this was before I had resigned at the hospital, I was under major stress and had little to no patience. It was not easy working with me at that time. James once threatened to quit if "this was the way I was going to be acting." It wasn't a pretty picture at all.

By the time help came, I was ready to drop. The first clue came when I hired an adult female, a mother of four, to help wait tables. Lisa G. came down that December and said she felt God sending her to help and was hired. Seeing the difference in how she handled the customers and how the teenagers did that was an eye opener. I began praying that God send me some women. Lisa introduced me to Lori D. who had worked for over twenty years at another restaurant in town. Lori became the ice pick that God used to help chip away at my walls, while I returned the favor. It was iron sharpening iron. The first six months were rough and she considered quitting and several times; I was ready to fire her. You wouldn't know it now as we are great friends and she is still working for me. She provided the help I needed at a crucial time because business definitely began to pick up.

Lori and I cooked in the morning, and then she took off her aprons and waited tables, while I fixed the plates. After lunch we continued cooking until she had to go pick up her children. After which she returned to the cafe, helped set up the steam table, and waited tables for dinner while I handled the back end cooking and fixing plates.

Now we laugh about how insane we had to be. Cooking with only two electric burners, burning food in the Vulcan pizza oven because it was too hot, trying to serve lunch when we didn't have enough time to prepare for dinner. Craziness! We were so tired and worn out that the thought of this continuing was a bit of a stretch. I would go home on Saturday night and simply drop. For months I lost Sundays because I was so exhausted I could not move out of the bed. If I did I moved to the floor and remained there for the entire day; never leaving the house.

Jimmy was equally exhausted. He was the dishwasher and, at that time, it was all by hand in the three bay sink. He also was the sweet potato peeler and cutter, the collard green cleaner and picker, in addition to all the paper work, payroll, and other administrative duties he did.

Eventually, God sent more competent women to wait tables and help with cleaning and making sure the cafe ran smoothly. They also had good rapport with the customers and added that down-to-earth feeling and hospitality that was our aim.

It was good timing because things really began moving pretty fast. People were calling and wanting to have their special dinners and celebrations at the cafe. I began experimenting with different entrees, spices, desserts, and gumbos and enjoying it. Basically, I was teaching myself how to cook on the job. It was evident that I had to add more selections to my menu and broaden my own cooking experience. My instruction came from cookbooks, magazines, Great Chefs of America, and eventually The Food Network. My inspiration came from God and my love of cooking from watching my mother in our home. My school was my kitchen, as my mother had never made Creole or Cajun recipes at home. But my first entrees were inspired by her like Momma's Lasagna which was her recipe; as well as coconut cake, fried chicken, rice puddings, squash casserole, corn pudding, fried fish, cornbread, collard greens, lamb, and the knowledge of fresh ingredients from having been raised on our small farm.

I was surprised that I had a talent for mixing spices and combining fruits with poultry or making Jamaican Jerk chicken using my own recipe for the jerk marinade; using fresh mango and pineapples, sometimes papaya salsas. I was fascinated with the fresh herbs and dark spices like cloves, nutmeg, allspice, cinnamon, coriander, and cumin when mixed with brown sugar or lemon and limejuices, fresh ginger, and fresh herbs. I created Moroccan lamb dishes using the dark spices, coconut milk, coriander, and fresh squeezed oranges or braised lamb shanks with citrus and spices. I gave my own flavor to meatloaf and created my famous BBQ Meatloaf with Monterey Jack cheese. I made my own

Jambalaya and Gumbo using fresh herbs, making a rich stock in which to fill with onions, peppers, celery, Creole spices, with lots of love and sausages. And for the first time I learned how to prepare fish and seafood entrees, such as shrimp and crab cakes, seafood chowders, seafood gumbos, salmon with fresh tropical salsas, fried catfish with spicy tomato sauce, or a Maine favorite - fried haddock. Then came pork loins and pork chops stuffed with Andouille sausage and sweet potato cornbread stuffing, or jerk pork tenderloin with a Cuban black bean and sweet potato sauce. And don't forget the BBQ bourbon baby back ribs marinated in my own creation of ingredients and covered with bourbon BBQ sauce. The men love them! And they are finger-lickin' good!

My mother's kitchen was an eclectic one, just like the cafe. Along with the beans and fried chicken came the spiced chicken with polenta, lasagna, and lamb dishes. I love surprising my customers each week because my menu changes weekly. Some things are almost always there like the ribs, macaroni and cheese, and collard greens. The rest I plan and create as I go. Our customers love it.

The recipes in this book are authentic and come from my kitchen but please remember most of the time I cook by feel and taste. I call it "vibration cooking" or "cooking with my soul." I taste and cook, throwing in the pot what I feel will work, whether savory or sweet. It is instinct, a gift, so please don't expect perfection from these recipes, but perfect them to your taste. I always start with a recipe book but I end up creating my own dish.

From the beginning, we've been blessed by God with excellent exposure beginning with word-of-mouth from lots of satisfied customers who went out and spread the word about Freedom Cafe. Then the feature article with recipes entitled "Thanksgiving with Soul," printed on November 21, 1999 introduced us to a lot of people. In January of 2002, we were featured on Made in Maine, a PBS cooking show with Lou McNally. In this show, our cafe was exposed to thousands of people in the state of Maine. Lou McNally and I cooked catfish, Jambalaya, Jerk pork tenderloin while we chatted and discussed Cajun and Creole cooking. In June of that same year, Down East Magazine featured us in their "Dining Out" section. One of their writers came to the cafe and had dinner without us knowing, obviously. She called the next week and told us she had eaten there, enjoyed the atmosphere, the service, and the food, especially the crab cakes, and wanted to feature us in Down East and finally Maine Food and

Lifestyle Magazine featured the café 2006. Of course I said, "Yes!" She came and interviewed us and wrote an excellent article, which again exposed us to tourists and Mainers as well. That summer we received a call from Peter McHegan of Boston Chronicles Television show, who was, at that time, doing a show about Maine. He wanted to feature our Creole restaurant on this show. Again, "Yes!" was the answer. They came and interviewed us, cameras and all, and the segment appeared that September.

This exposure brought customers in from all around the state and, in the summer, tourists. And during the summer of 2003, Hollywood came to town in the form of the "Empire Falls" movie stars and crew. Freedom Cafe was one of the restaurants that the crew particularly ate at, as well as a handful of the stars, specifically William Fichtner, Aiden Quinn, and Ed Harris. One night Mr. Fichtner came in and I didn't know who he was, but treated him as I would all my customers. It was late and I had turkey and dressing on the menu. He ordered a plate of turkey and dressing and a piece of my fried chicken. I loaded his plate up sky high and told him to "enjoy," which is customary for me.

He finished eating and called me over to his table to show that he not only enjoyed the food, but had cleaned his plate. Later, when he came in with the others, I knew who he was. He was very nice and kind to us, always talking with the staff and getting to know them. When interviewed by the Morning Sentinel he actually mentioned Freedom Cafe. Fichtner (William) appears to be, in fact, a very affable person who said he is thoroughly enjoying Maine, its residents and the food. 'The Freedom Café (in Waterville) is fantastic, the food, and the atmosphere.' (Morning Sentinel, September 10, 2003). While we appreciate all the publicity and free exposure, the one thing that keeps Freedom Cafe in business is word-of-mouth, customers that continue to come and bring others.

The Rumor

After the third customer asked me if we "still cooked the food elsewhere and brought it to the café", my response was almost impatient when I stated, "We have always cooked all of our food on premise, and never cooked it elsewhere", right Lori?" Turning to Lori Dumont, who has worked with me over ten years, who respond; "That's right." It was an insult to me because as hard and long as I work in the kitchen to make sure things are fresh and make by my own hands, and my dessert chef Amanda Kelly. It was hard to hear that this rumor had been circulating for quite some time.

I am not sure where the rumor started or who started it, but even down on Silver Street we cooked on premise in that big pizza oven and electric stove, before getting the eight burner gas stove that changed our lives forever.

Today, as always, most of the food is prepped and cooked on the days that we are open and serve it – and all is prepped in our kitchen, cooked in our kitchen, and served from our kitchen. We don't cook food on Monday and reheat and serve it on Thursday. The fact is we go through food fast, which is good, which means we are continuing to prep it fresh and cook it throughout the weekend.

"So, for all of you who thought or heard that we cooked our food elsewhere and then brought it into the café – it's not true."

Seafood

Growing up we caught small crappies in the ponds in Mississippi. I loved fishing but haven't done much since I married at the age of 18. The fish we caught we scaled, seasoned with cornmeal, salt and pepper, and fried in a large cast iron skillet. These hand-sized fishes were full of small bones which made eating them hazardous but good, with hushpuppies, fries and syrup for breakfast.

Before moving to Maine and opening the café I had never eaten seafood so learning to prepare shrimp and crab cakes and the other recipes in this section was again, on the job training, an adventure into a food place that I had not traveled before. I knew that I needed to add seafood to my menu and there are no crappies here, and Maine is about seafood, although I never conquered the lobster I did come up with a few good seafood dishes. Enjoy!

SHRIMP & CRAB CAKES W/ FRESH MANGO SALSA

1 lb shrimp, clean, deveined, tail off
2 lbs crabmeat, fresh
¼ Red onion, chopped
½ Red pepper, chopped
½ Orange pepper, chopped
2 T. fresh basil, chopped
2 T. fresh parsley, chopped
1 tsp Creole seasoning
1-1/2 tsp garlic powder
1-1/2 tsp onion powder
1 T. garlic, minced
1 lemon juiced and zest
1 8 oz box of Progresso Italian Panko Crumbs
¼ cup heavy Cream
½ cup sour cream
3 eggs

Thaw shrimp, set aside; check crabmeat for cartilage and shell; in a food processor chop red onion, peppers, basil and parsley together until finely chopped; in a bowl place chopped veggies and herbs, garlic, lemon juice and zest along with crabmeat, mix well. In the same food processor place half of the thawed shrimp in the food processor, add eggs and heavy cream and sour cream and blend until it resembles a mousse and the shrimp is finely ground. Add the mousse into the bowl with the rest of the spices, then chop the remainder of shrimp in food processor, add to bow. Then add panko crumbs, gently mix until well blended. Using a large ice cream scoop, form into cakes. Spoon into your hand and began making cakes the size you want. If the cakes are not tight enough, simply add more Panko crumbs.

Heat a nonstick skillet, covering the bottom with oil, and began to sauté cakes until golden brown; place on a cookie sheet and finish in a heated oven of 350 degrees until done through, about fifteen minutes. Top with mango salsa and enjoy. This makes about 20 cakes, depending on your size; servings 10 (two cakes per serving).

MANGO COCONUT PINEAPPLE SALSA

3 – 4 fresh mangoes, peeled and chopped
1 can of pineapples chunks or fresh pineapple cut up in small chunks
½ red onion, chopped
½ red pepper, chopped
½ cup chopped green scallions
4 T. Crème de Coconut (sweet)
1 Lemon, juiced with zest
2 T of chopped fresh parsley or cilantro

Prep ingredients and place all in a bowl and mix well; season to taste. Refrigerate until ready to use. This Salsa is good on any fish or chicken.

SOUTHERN FRIED CATFISH W/ ANDOUILLE CREAM SAUCE

Catfish, boneless, skinless fillets
Louisiana Fish Seasoning
2 T. Creole Spices
1 T. Lemon Pepper
1 T. each Onion & Garlic Powder

Mix fish seasonings and spices together in a container large enough to bread catfish fillets;

In a large frying skillet heat two inches of oil until hot, until it sizzles when you throw a little seasoning mix into it; carefully add breaded catfish fillets, laying into the hot oil to prevent splashing hot oil. Fish cooks about 3-4 minutes on each side; drain on paper towel; serve hot, with either mango pineapple salsa or Andouille cream sauce.

This seasoning mix can be used for any fish you wish to fry including tilapia and haddock.

ANDOUILLE CREAM SAUCE

2 – 3 cups of chopped Andouille sausages or any spicy sausage
½ onions chopped
1 stick butter
2 cups Heavy Cream

1 cup of Chicken broth
2 pkg. Hollandaise Paste or Powder
2 T. each of Garlic, Onion Powder
3 T. chopped fresh parsley
3 T. chopped fresh Basil
½ lemon juice and zest

If your smoked sausages has a dark casing, peel off, cut links in half and then into fourths. Head a heavy gauge sauce pan and butter and a little oil to keep from burning; add sausages and onions and sautéed until juices are coming out of sausages and onions are sweating. Add chicken broth and heat; then add paste or powder whisking constantly as it will begin to thicken; add heavy cream then add lemon and zest, spices and fresh herbs. Wisk until thicken. Serve hot over fried chicken or fish. It is great gravy for grits as well.

CREOLE STUFFED HADDOCK

4 6-8 ounces of boneless, skinless haddock fillets
Old Bay Seasoning for Fish
Lemon Pepper

Stuffing
12 oz fresh crab meat
½ stick of melted butter
2 T. fresh lemon juice with zest
½ cup heavy Cream
½ cup sour cream

1/3 cup green scallions, chopped
1/3 red pepper, chopped
1 T. minced garlic
Fresh parsley, chopped
2 cup Panko bread crumbs
1 T. Creole spices
½ stick of melted butter
½ cup White wine

Season the haddock fillets with old bay seasoning and lemon pepper; then place in a buttered ramekin or casserole dish. Mix stuffing ingredients together, season with Creole spices, then place stuffing on top of haddock; then pour melted butter and wine over haddock; bake at 350 degrees, uncovered, until crispy on top and fish is done and flaky about 30 minutes.

SHRIMP ETTOUFFEE

2 lbs peeled, deveined, tail off shrimp
½ stick of butter
4 T. vegetable oil
1 sweet onion, chopped
2 peppers, red and green, chopped
½ cup chopped celery
3 Tbsp. each of fresh chopped parsley and basil
2 cups chopped spicy sausages, Kielbasa, Beef Smoked, etc.
2 cans diced tomatoes

1 bottle of Lawry's Caribbean Jerk Sauce
1 can crushed pineapples w/ juice
2 cups of chicken stock
1/3 cup brown sugar
3 T. Creole Seasonings, Zataran's
2 T. garlic powder and onion powder

If shrimp is frozen thaw; meanwhile in a skillet melt the butter with oil, then add onion, peppers, celery and garlic; after vegetables soften add chopped sausages and cooked until slightly brown; then add tomatoes, pineapples, sugar, jerk sauce, herbs, and the rest of the spices and ingredients; cook until combined and hot. Then add shrimp last and cook until done. If you like it spicy add hot pepper sauce to taste. If it is too thick add more chicken stock. Serve over hot rice. Serves 6 to 8.

SIDES

COLLARD GREENS

20 cups cleaned and cut up collard greens
4 quarts of water (cover greens)
2 smoked turkey wings or drumsticks or 2 smoked ham hocks
1 tsp crushed red pepper flakes
4 T. salt
1 T. black pepper
4 T. garlic powder
4 T. onion powder
¼ cup minced garlic
¼ cup apple cider vinegar
½ cup Worcestershire
1 cup brown sugar
¼ cup canola oil
2 ounces of Liquid Smoke

In a large stock pot place water, smoked turkey or ham hocks (both if you like) and the rest of the ingredients except the collard greens. Bring ingredients to a boil, boil for about ten minutes, and add the collard greens in small batches to allow them to cook down then add the rest. Cook until tender — about two hours; an hour into cooking, taste and adjust seasonings if necessary. Yields 8-10 servings. Enjoy!

FREEDOM CAFÉ'S MACARONI & CHEESE

4 cups cooked elbow macaroni
1 stick of melted butter
3 cups of mozzarella/smoked provolone cheese
3 cups yellow cheddar, mild or sharp
1 cup of Colby/jack
4 cups whole milk
1 cup heavy cream
1 cup sour cream
1 cup cottage cheese
2 tablespoon each of garlic powder, onion powder
1 teaspoon Lawry's seasoning salt
1 teaspoon of black pepper

In a bowl mix cooked macaroni, melted butter and blend well; add sour cream and cottage cheese, mix well; then add cream and milk with cheese and mix well; adjust seasoning to your taste then pour into a baking disk; bake on 375 until bubbly and cheese is melted, 30-45 minutes; serves 8 to 10.

To add more kick to macaroni, take Ritz cracker crumbs and mix with melted butter and topped the casserole before baking.

CORNBREAD

1 cup yellow cornmeal
2 cup all purpose flour (or two cups of yellow Duncan Hines cake mix)
2 T. baking powder
½ cup granulated sugar
1 tsp. salt
½ cup vegetable oil
2 cups whole milk or buttermilk
3 eggs
2 T. oil for skillet or pan

In a mixing bowl place all your dry ingredients and stir well; add whole milk, eggs and oil, and stir until well incorporated. If mix is too stiff or dry, add more milk until it looks like cake batter. Then take 2 tablespoons of oil and grease a cast iron skillet or baking pan, pour batter into pan.

At this point you can add a can of drained Mexican corn; chopped broccoli, onions and sharp cheddar cheese; or fry some bacon, drained, break into pieces and add to the batter with ½ cup of sour cream). Bake in a preheated oven at 350 degrees, for about ½ hour until done – test the middle.

While baking take ½ cup of honey and ½ stick of butter and melt in a bowl in the microwave; as soon as cornbread comes out of the oven brush mixture over the cornbread; cut and enjoy.

SUCCOTASH

1 bag frozen or fresh lima beans
1 bag of frozen or fresh corn (or 2 cans Mexican corn)
2 yellow squash, fresh, cut up in bite-size pieces
2 zucchini squash, fresh cut up in bite-size piece
2 cans of seasoned diced tomatoes
2 T. minced garlic
½ bunch fresh parsley, chopped
½ cup sugar
1 T. dry oregano
1 T. dry basil
1 T. dry thyme
1 stick butter, melted
2 T. garlic powder
2 T. onion powder
2 tsp. Black pepper

Chop vegetables, placed in a casserole pan large enough to hold all of the ingredients; mix everything together well, then add the butter, melted, cover with foil and bake in a preheated 400 degree oven about 45 minutes, stirring once midway through, until it melds together and is tender and lima beans soft.

SOUR CREAM MASHED POTATOES

5 lbs of Yukon gold potatoes, peeled
2 sticks butter, melted
1 cup sour cream
1 cup heavy cream
3 T. minced garlic
2 T. onion powder
2 T. garlic powder
1 T. black pepper
4 T. fresh chopped parsley or chives
Salt to taste

Boil potatoes until fork tender in salted water;

Drain and mashed potatoes while hot; then add butter, sour cream and heavy cream, mashed and blend well with a hand held electric beaters or by hand; then add the rest of the seasonings; adjust to your taste.

POPPY SEED COLESLAW

2 small bags of Coleslaw Mix (Cabbage/Carrots)
1 to 2 bottles of Maries Poppy Seed Dressing
2 Granny Smith Apple (chopped)
½ cup of craisins
½ up of pecans
¼ cup sugar
(1 tsp cinnamon optional)

Prep and chopped apples, mix all ingredients together in a bowl until everything well incorporated. If you would like to keep your apples white, place them in a bowl of water with some lemon juice until you mix them in.

GRITS & SAUSAGE CASSEROLE

5 cups cooked Quick Grits (follow directions on box)
2 cups of spicy turkey or any sausages, browned and drained
1 stick butter
1 cup chopped green pepper
1 cup chopped onions
1 cup finely chopped celery
2 cups cheddar cheese
1 cup Parmesan cheese
2 cups whole milk
Season with 1 T. each of onion powder, garlic powder, black pepper
Add salt if needed.

Once you have cooked the grits in a large pot, then add butter, green pepper, onions, celery and milk, mix well, then add sausages, cheeses and seasoning, mix well. If grits are too thick, add additional milk until creamy.

Spoon into casserole and bake on 350 degrees until cheese is melted, veggies soft.

SWEET RELISH POTATO SALAD

I love my potato salad sweet with the taste of pickles. During our family reunions, picnics and BBQs my job was to bring the potato salad. This is the recipe. It goes well with the BBQ chicken.

8 cups diced potatoes (your choice)
8 cups water
1 T. salt
2 eggs

Place all ingredients in a stockpot and boil until potatoes are tender and eggs are done. Drain and place potatoes in bowl. Peel and chop eggs. Add the following and mix well.

1 cup mayonnaise
1 cup sweet pickle relish
3 T. mustard
1 cup onions, chopped
2 eggs, chopped
1 T. black pepper
1 T. onion powder
1 T. garlic powder

Basically, season to taste using your favorite herbs and spices.

CANDIED YAMS

8 cups sliced fresh sweet potatoes (6-8 large)
3 cups brown sugar
2 cups white sugar
½ stick of butter
2 T. cinnamon
1 T. nutmeg
2 T. vanilla extract

Place all of the ingredients in medium sized pot and boil until potatoes are fork tender and syrupy. You can add orange juice, pumpkin spice seasonings to take the flavor to different level.

CREAM OF SWEET POTATO SOUP

Make candied yams (above) pour 1/2 of the juice off into a measuring cup.

½ cup whole or minced garlic, roast in olive oil in a skillet on top of the stove, stirring constantly until garlic is brown but not burnt.

Take an emersion blender or blend in a food processor the yams and garlic until smooth; then add 1 cup of heavy cream, 1 cup of chicken stock; add salt and pepper to taste; additionally I usually add small amounts of nutmeg, cinnamon, allspice, garlic and onion powder, then blend well. If soup is too thick either add more stock or cream; reheat on the stove; serve and enjoy.

HOPPIN' JOHNS (BLACK-EYED PEAS)

4 quarts of water
2 ham hocks (or smoked turkey)
2 cup diced smoked sausages
2 cups chopped onions
2 cups chopped green peppers
2 28 oz cans of diced tomatoes (basil, oregano, garlic) Hunts
¼ cup Worcestershire sauce
2 16 oz dry black-eyed peas (checked for stones) rinsed
3 T. minced garlic
2 T. garlic powder
2 T. onion powder
1 T. black pepper
3 T. Creole seasonings
1 T. dried thyme
1 T. dried oregano

In a medium sized pot, place water, ham hocks (or smoked turkey), chopped vegetables, tomatoes and spices, and let boil for five minutes, then add black-eyed peas and cook on low until tender and tasty. These peas scorch easily as when they cook down they thicken; so stir often and add additional stock or water if needed; cook on medium low for 1-2 hours.

Optional is to serve over rice, and add diced ham or smoked sausages to the pot in the beginning for additional flavor. Enjoy!

SUMMER SQUASH CASSEROLE

Dinnertime at our house meant we all ate together with few exceptions. At each meal we had to wait until everyone was at the table before we ate. Whether it was during the week when all we had were white navy beans with catsup, cornbread cooked in a cast iron skillet, and fried chicken, or on Saturday when homemade lasagna or chicken polenta was served. Summer meant we had lots of fresh vegetables from our garden, like the summer squash casserole. We didn't touch the food until everyone was gathered and each one said a prayer. Since I was always in a hurry to get to eating, my prayer was simple and to the point. "Jesus wept." Let's eat.

6 large summer (yellow) squash
½ cup flour
Salt
1T. black pepper
½ onions sliced

1 tsp salt
½ *stick* butter
8 T. sugar
3 eggs
1 cup half-and-half

Wash squash and cut off the ends. Place in a medium sized pot and fill with water with a pinch of salt. When squash becomes fork tender, drain in colander, and stir squash to break it up and allow the excess water to drain. Leave for five minutes. When well drained, place in mixing bowl and add butter, onion, eggs, flour, pepper, salt, sugar, and half-and-half. Mix all the ingredients well. Pour mixture into a buttered casserole and bake at 350 degrees for 25 minutes until done. Serves around 4.

LIMA BEANS PLAIN & GOOD

2.5 lbs fresh or frozen baby lima beans
8 cups water
½ *stick* butter
1 T. salt
2 T. onion powder
1. T. black pepper

Place beans in a medium sized pot. Add the water, butter, salt and pepper, and onion powder. Cook on high heat for 15 minutes Reduce heat to a rolling boil for another 15 minutes until water has reduced to make a thick sauce and beans are soft. Enjoy with a slice of corn bread with honey butter and candied yams.

DESSERTS

PECAN BOURBON CHOCOLATE CHIP PIE

3 eggs
1/8 t. salt
1 cup Karo light corn syrup
1-1/2 cup pecans
1 cup sugar
1/2 cup semi-sweet chocolate chips
2 T. melted butter
9 inch unbaked pie shell
1 T. vanilla extract
2 T. bourbon

With an electric mixer, beat eggs until slightly blended, add syrup, sugar, vanilla, salt, melted butter and bourbon and mix well. In unbaked pie shell, layer pecans and chocolate chips; pour pie mixture over pecans and chocolate. Bake in a preheated oven at 400 degrees for 45 minutes to an hour or until the middle is slightly giggly but firm.

CHOCOLATE PEANUT BUTTER PIE

1 Oreo Cookie Crust
8 oz Cream Cheese, softened
5 oz creamy peanut butter, with or without chunks
1 T. Vanilla
2 – 4 T. Heavy Cream
4 T. Hershey's Chocolate Syrup
1 cup confectioner's sugar

In an electric mixer blend softened cream cheese until fluffy; add peanut butter and blend well; then add vanilla, heavy cream, chocolate syrup, confectioner's sugar, and continue to mix on med-high speed until it lightens in color and is fluffy. Spoon the mixture into Oreo cookie crust and smooth out. On top add your choice or Reese's pieces, chocolate chips and peanut butter chips. Chill 4- 8 hours or overnight; serves 8.

Jimmy's Favorite Banana Pudding

The next few recipes are dishes that I prepared in the early years of our marriage, Jimmy really loved banana pudding. Don't be surprised that I'm using a box pudding because this pudding is rich and full of flavor, creamy and delicious.

6 bananas, sliced
1 box of Vanilla Wafers (12 oz)
1 can sweetened condensed milk
2 cups heavy cream (cold)
3 boxes of Jell-O Instant Banana Cream Pudding (3.4 oz boxes)
3 cups whole milk (cold)

Using an electric or handheld mixer, pour the can of sweetened condensed milk, two cups of heavy cream in mixing bowl and blend for about two minutes, just to incorporate well. Add boxes of pudding and 2 cups of whole milk, blend until the mixture begins to get creamy and begins to thicken. Using six 16-oz. ramekins or a medium sized glass casserole dish - layer vanilla wafers on the bottom and up along the side; then layer sliced bananas and top with a even layer of pudding mix; repeat by layering vanilla wafers, bananas, and pudding; decorate top with left-over cookies; refrigerate until ready to eat or just eat.

CAROLYN'S SEVEN UP CAKE

3 sticks of unsalted butter, room temperature
2-3/4 cups of sugar
5 eggs
1 tsp salt
2 tbs lemon extract
1 lemon, juiced and zested
3 cups cake flour
¾ cup of seven up (soda)

Using an electric mixer or hand held, cream room temperature butter and sugar; add lemon extract, juice and zest; mix well then add eggs one at a time until incorporated; then add flour and mix well. Fold the seven-up into batter until blended. Pour in a butter and floured Bundt cake pan; bake in a preheated oven at 325 degrees for 1-1/2 hours until toothpick comes out clean.

This cake is excellent with coffee; or sliced and served with fresh fruit and lemon glaze. You can make the glaze with fresh lemon juice, butter and confectioner's sugar, stir over medium heat until incorporated – sweeten to your taste.

JANICE'S PECAN PRALINES

1 cup white sugar
1 cup brown sugar
1 tsp. salt
½ stick butter
½ cup heavy cream
1-1/2 cup pecan halves
1 T. vanilla extract

Measure out all your ingredients before you begin. Cover a cookie sheet place wax paper that is generously buttered. Have a candy thermometer handy. I always use a wooden spoon to stir the candy.

Using heavy gauge sauce pan add sugars, cream, butter and began to stir ingredients well. Stir constantly until mixture thickens and begins to bubble. Place candy thermometer in mix until it reaches 238 degrees. Take pan off add vanilla, salt, and pecans, stirring quickly. Then spoon onto buttered wax paper. Let harden then enjoy. Makes about one dozen small pralines.

COCONUT CAKE

2 – ¾ cups all purpose flour
1 t. baking powder
1 t. baking soda
1-3/4 cups granulated sugar
½ t. salt
2 sticks of butter, room temperature
1 can cream of coconut, sweetened (Goya)
4 large eggs, separated
1 cup buttermilk
1 T. vanilla extract
Cream Cheese Frosting
Sweetened Coconut Flakes

Mix all dry ingredients in a bowl, blending well. Separate eggs taking egg whites and whipping them into soft peaks, set aside.

In an electric mixer bowl cream sugar, butter and coconut cream and vanilla until well blended. Then add egg yolks blending in one at a time until mixed well; then add flour mixture and buttermilk in two increments. After well mixed fold in the egg whites, do not beat with electric mixture, fold. Then pour batter in three floured and greased cake pans with wax paper. Bake in a preheated oven at 350 degrees until cake rises and a toothpick comes out clean. Cool on cake rack. Remove cakes, frost then and place flakes to frosting.

WHITE CHOCOLATE BREAD PUDDING W/ BOURBON SAUCE

10 croissants (sandwich sized)
4 eggs
2-1/2 cups sugar
1 qt of heavy cream
3 cups whole milk
2 Tbs. Vanilla extract
1 ½ cups of craisins
2 oz melted butter

Take a sauce pan and add additional heavy cream and 2 cups of white chocolate chips, stirring constantly until chocolate is melted: set aside.

In a large-bowl cut or tear croissants into bite-size pieces; then add eggs, milk and heavy cream, and butter; add sugar, vanilla extract and cranberries or craisins, mix well; then add melted white chocolate chips and cream, mix well. Pour into a greased 2 inch deep round pans or a casserole (two); can freeze one. Then bake in a preheated 350 degree oven for 45 minutes to an hour; or until puddings rise up and pudding is firm.

Bourbon Sauce:

1 lb brown sugar
1 stick of butter

1 T. vanilla extract
½ cup of bourbon
1 ½ cups of heavy cream

For the Bourbon sauce in a heavy gauge sauce pan melt butter, brown sugar and heavy cream; stir until butter is melted and mixture is smooth and creamy; remove sauce pan from flame and then add bourbon, place back on the heat and stir until bourbon is well blended; serve on cooked bread pudding.

In 2003 I went to New Orleans with Jeri Roseboro a friend of mine. She went attending a work related seminar; I went for the purpose of trying recipes and eating at Emeril's and Paul Prudhomme's restaurants; and attending the New Orleans School of Cooking. It was nice trying to well-known restaurants but my favorite meal was at the hotel on the final day of our stay. There, at lunch, we were served "White Chocolate Bread Pudding with Bourbon Sauce." It was soooo good that I went back into the kitchen and asked the chef if he would give it to me; after all, I was in Maine and he in New Orleans; there's no competition there. He was so kind to share it with me, and over the years I've shared it with a few people, including Richard, but now I get to share it with all of my customers. Here's to the "White Chocolate Bread Pudding" with Bourbon sauce.

Dear Janice, I'm the fellow from Montana who begged you for your bread pudding recipe. I sat at the bar with my wife. Thank you so much for sharing your recipe with me! I made it last night for an evening with friends and you're now their new best friend. I gave you full credit, but I refused to give them the recipe. Thanks again. Richard

FROZEN MOCHA PIE

16 ounces of cream cheese (softened)
1 can sweetened condensed milk
3 tsp vanilla extract
16 ounces cool whip
2 tablespoons instant coffee granules (dissolve in 2 T. warm water)
8 ounces chocolate syrup (1 cup)
8 cups of Oreo cookies, chopped or broken into small pieces
1 cup of chopped pecans
4 Oreo cookie pie crusts

In an electric mixer whipped cream cheese until soft and fluffy; add condensed milk, vanilla extract and blend until well incorporated. Then add the chocolate and blend well. Remove bowl and fold in (with spatula or spoon) cool whip, then fold in pecans and Oreo cookie crumbs; blend well and spoon into pie crusts. Freeze overnight or at least 8 hours until set. Slice and serve. This makes four pies; leave the rest in the freezer for the rest of the summer or half the recipe and make two.

One of the first desserts that we made at Freedom Café came from the ladies in the small café at Maine General Hospital. When I worked there I would break there and one of the ladies heard that I was opening a café and gave me this recipe. It is very nice in the summer and was very popular in the beginning of the restaurant.

SWEET POTATO CHEESE CAKE

1/4 cup butter or margarine, melted
1/4 cup sugar
1-3/4 cups graham cracker crumbs
2 medium sweet potatoes, baked and peeled
Two 8-ounce packages cream cheese
3/4 cup sugar
2 eggs
1/4 cup orange liqueur or orange juice
1 teaspoon ground cinnamon
1/8 teaspoon ground cloves
Pinch nutmeg
1 teaspoon vanilla
1 cup sour cream
Whipped cream, sweetened

Mix butter, sugar, and graham cracker crumbs and press into bottom and up sides of a 9-inch spring form pan. Bake 10 minutes at 350 degrees. In a large mixing bowl, beat sweet potatoes until smooth. Add cream cheese and beat until blended. Add remaining ingredients except whipped cream and beat until well mixed. Pour into cooled crust and bake at 350 degrees for 50 minutes. Store in refrigerator but let stand at room temperature for about 30 minutes before serving. Serve with whipped cream.

KEY LIME PIE

1 graham cracker crust
3 egg yolks
1 lime zest
1 14-ounce can sweetened condensed milk
2/3 cup of freshly squeezed or bottled lime juice
(regular limes)

In an electric mixer place egg yolks and lime zest blend until yolks become a pale yellow and fluffy. Gradually add the condensed milk and continue to beat on medium speed until thick, 3 to 4 minutes. Lower the speed and slowly pour lime juice and zest into the mixture until combined. Pour into the graham crust and bake for ten minutes until filling set. Cool and refrigerate until ready to serve. Slice and top with whipped cream.

LEMON ICE BOX PIE

1 8 oz cream cheese, room temperature
1 cup fresh squeezed lemon juice
Zest of 1 lemon
1 can of sweetened condensed milk
1 T. vanilla extract
1 graham cracker crust

In mixer or with hand held mixer, beat cream cheese and condensed milk until light and fluffy, scraping bowl to incorporate cream cheese. Gradually pour lemon juice and zest, and vanilla extract. Blend on medium speed until the mixture thickens. Pour into graham crust and chill until set – 4 hours or overnight.

PEACH COBBLER

4 cans peaches in heavy syrup
½ stick of butter
2 cups sugar mixed with ½ cup of cornstarch
2 T. nutmeg
2 T. cinnamon
1 lemon juiced and zest
1 T. vanilla

Topping:
4 cups bisquick mix
1 cup brown sugar
1 stick of butter, melted
1 T. Vanilla extract
1 tsp. nutmeg
1 tsp. cinnamon
2 cups half n half

In a thick bottom sauce pan add peaches, drain two cans, and add two cans with syrup; heat and melt butter, adding the sugar blend and spices, vanilla and lemon juice. Stir until mixture thickens.

Mix all of the ingredients of the topping in a bowl, it should resemble a batter. Pour peach mixture in a baking dish, spoon topping over peaches. Bake in a preheated oven at 400 degrees until topping is cooked through and brown. Serve with a scoop of vanilla ice cream or homemade whipped cream.

GRETCHEN'S STRAWBERRY CAKE

1 box of strawberry cake mix
1 box of strawberry Jell-O
4 eggs
2 tablespoons of flour
½ cup of cold water
½ cup of frozen strawberries with juice

Glaze:
½ cup of strawberries (fresh or frozen)
½ stick of butter
¾ to 1 box of confectioner's sugar

In an electric mixer mix all ingredients and beat for 4 minutes. Bake in a greased and flour Bundt pan or regular cake pans (2) for 50 minutes, using toothpick to test if done. Mix glaze and pour over warm cake. (Optional is to take a fork and make holes in cake, pour glaze so that it infiltrates the cake, making it more flavorful.

Gretchen's husband, Neil, who is a very thoughtful and extremely in touch man, called and requested this cake for his wife's birthday. It was the cake that her mother always made for her birthdays. He sent the recipe via email and Amanda made it. The original recipe called for white cake mix but we chose Duncan Hines Strawberry Cake mix. We made it for her birthday. She and her mother and family came in to celebrate her birthday. She and her mom were very surprised when we presented it. Nonetheless, we served it to our customers and they loved it as well, and several of you have requested it, so here it is. Like the gingerbread recipe following, was requested by one of our customers, just as I was completing the cookbook.

GINGERBREAD APPLE CAKE

2-1/2 cups all purpose flour
1 tsp ground allspice
½ tsp freshly ground black pepper
1-½ tsp powdered ginger
1 cup light brown sugar
1 cup unsulfured molasses
2 eggs, lightly beaten
1 cup canola oil
2 tsp. baking soda
1 cup boiling water
4 T. peeled fresh ginger, grated

Sift together first 4 ingredients and set aside. Mix sugar, molasses, eggs and oil. Add dry ingredients. In the boiling water add soda, let rise, then add to gingerbread batter; add fresh ginger, mix well then pour over the apple pie filling.

2 bags of apples, Cortland, Fuji, etc. mix your favorites
3 T. fresh lemon juice
2 cups packed brown sugar
1 stick butter
3 T. vanilla extract
3 T. cinnamon

½ tsp. Allspice
2 tsp. Nutmeg

Peel and slice apples, cook in a heavy gauge pan; add the remaining ingredients and cook down until apples are soft; pour in the bottom of baking dish; then add the gingerbread batter on top; bake in a preheated oven at 350 degree for 50 minutes or until toothpick comes out clean.

5/31/08

Dear Janice

I just finished reading your book yesterday. I am amazed and awestruck about your life story.

*What most impressed me was your seeking after God. I would challenge you in your thought that you have not explored God in Maine as **you** planned. Maybe from your perspective, but from my view, I believe you have explored and experienced, and are experiencing God the way **He** planned for your life. Your truth and honesty are so uplifting. I found myself crying at the end of several of the chapters. The one about healing and how it hurts more right before complete healing. I prayed for my own healing from hurts. I get the relationship with you and your Mom! (Me, too!)*

God is so faithful and good and merciful. I am so glad you and James are in Maine. Your "Freedom Café" is always a "balm" to our weary souls.

Many Blessings – Julie R.

Entrees

COCONUT CURRY CHICKEN W/ FRESH GRAPES (WEST AFRICAN COCONUT CHICKEN CURRY)

4 8 oz chicken breast, boneless, skinless
4 large boneless, skinless chicken thighs
Spice mix:
2 T. curry powder
2 T. orange peel
2 T. each garlic, onion powder
1 T. ground ginger
1 T. poultry seasonings
2 tsp allspice
2 T. chili powder
1 T. lemon pepper
3 T. brown sugar
3 T. flour

1 T. grated fresh ginger
2 T. minced garlic
1 small chopped white onion
1 small green pepper chopped

Thai Coconut Curry Broth (College Inn)
½ can of Cream of Coconut Milk (sweet)

2 cups green grapes, sliced or whole
2 cups sweetened coconut flakes

2 cups sliced almonds

Cut up chicken into bite-sized pieces; take the spice mix in a bowl, mix well then cover chicken in spices; in a hot skillet with about ¼ cup oil, sautéed seasoned chicken until brown. Remove chicken from skillet, sautéed onions, peppers, garlic and ginger for five minutes; add additional oil if need. Add curry broth and coconut milk. Add chicken to skillet, add grapes, coconut flakes and sliced almonds; additional curry and spices, as needed. Cook until chicken is tender, done, and sauce is thickened, about fifteen minutes. Served over rice. Serves 6 – 8.

BUTTERMILK FRIED CHICKEN

1 whole chicken, cut up
1 cup lemon juice
1 quart buttermilk
½ cup minced garlic

Place the above ingredients in a plastic bowl, massage liquids into chicken, seal tightly with plastic wrap and marinate overnight. Remove chicken from marinade and pat dry with paper towels. Set aside.

In a separate bowl mix:
4 cups flour
1 T. Lawry's Seasoning Salt

2 T. each of garlic powder, onion powder, lemon pepper

1 T. dried oregano

1 T. dried basil

1 T. dried thyme

Mix breading ingredients well, taste, and if you need more seasonings add. When flour is ready, coat chicken pieces thoroughly; set aside.

In a large cast iron or nonstick skillet pour 2 inches of oil; heat to frying stage; gently lay half of the chicken in the hot oil turning as it browns, at least twice; take chicken out and place on a sheet pan and finish cooking in a preheat 425 oven until 165 degrees on a thermometer. Take chicken out and serve hot.

CUBAN STYLE PORK TENDERLOIN W/ BLACK BEANS

2 pork tenderloins, trimmed

Spice Mix: ½ cup brown sugar, 2 T garlic powder, 2 T onion powder, 3 T minced garlic, 3 T five spice seasoning, 1 T salt, 1 T pepper. In a bowl mix well and using only half the mixture, rub tenderloins and refrigerate to allow seasoning in.

Cut pork in bite sized pieces and sautéed in hot skillet until brown, not completely cooked through.

Take pork out and add 2 cups chopped onions, 1 cup of chopped red and yellow peppers, fresh chopped parsley, the other half of the spice mix, 2 cans of black beans, 1 bottle of Iron Chef Orange Glaze with Ginger, 1bottle of Lawry's Caribbean jerk Marinade; add 2 tablespoons of fresh grated ginger, 2 cups of chicken stock, 1 bottle of tropical fruit mix, ½ cup of dark rum, one 2 T of lemon juice and zest, and reduce slightly, then add pork and cook through. Serve over rice.

PULLED PORK

1 large pork butt
8 oz orange juice
2 T. crushed red pepper
2 T. Lawry's Seasoning salt
3 T. onion powder
3 T. garlic powder
3 T. ground Chipotle
1 cup brown sugar
1 cup Worcestershire sauce
½ cup apple cider vinegar
½ cup minced garlic

Mix all ingredients in a bowl and rub and pour over pork butt; marinade overnight or 24 hours. Cook in preheated oven on 250 for 5 to 8 hours, turning every hour, until the pork is falling apart; with a knife and fork, pulled pork apart into bite size pieces. Using the left over pan juices, your favorite BBQ sauce; add a little apple cider vinegar, brown sugar, garlic and hot pepper sauce for "hog soppin" sauce. Cook sauce in pan and serve with pulled pork.

BEEF BRISKET

1 6-8 lb beef brisket, flat (trimmed preferred)

Spice Rub mix well:
3 T. Canadian Steak Seasoning
2 T. garlic and herbs
2 T. onion powder
1 T. salt
1 T. pepper

10 Garlic gloves
4 ounces Worcestershire
4 ounces beer
2 ounces liquid smoke
Fresh thyme

In a small bowl mix spices well; with a sharp knife make little slits in brisket, take gloves of garlic and hide in these little pockets; generously rub spice blend on brisket, all over, lay in pan with fat side up. Place 5 fresh thyme sprigs, the remainder of any garlic, pour beer, liquid smoke and Worcestershire sauce over brisket. Then wrap tightly in foil and bake in a 350 degree oven for three hours, until tender — check after two hours then continue baking another hour until fork tender and the temperature is 200 at least. Cool. Slice. You can serve this with our blue cheese herb butter or your favorite bbq sauce.

BLUE CHEESE HERB BUTTER

12 ounces of blue cheese crumbles
1 stick melted butter
2 tablespoons chopped each of fresh parsley, fresh basil
1 tablespoon of chopped fresh thyme (or your favorite)
2 tablespoons of minced garlic
2 tablespoons of steak seasoning (I use Montreal Steak)
¼ cup Worcestershire sauce

In a food processor or mixing bowl place cheese crumbles, melted butter and Worcestershire sauce, blend well; then add fresh herbs and seasoning, mix well, serve. This butter can be refrigerated for up to a week or more.

BBQ MEATLOAF WITH MONTEREY JACK CHEESE

1 lb lean ground beef (sirloin)
½ lb ground pork
½ lb ground beef chuck

2 pkgs. of Lipton Beefy Onion Soup
2 T. each of onion powder, garlic powder, Italian herbs,
3/4 c. brown sugar
1 c. chopped onions
1 c. chopped green peppers
1-2 c. honey smoke BBQ sauce (I use Kraft)
3/4 c. crushed pineapples
1/4 c. Worcestershire sauce
3 T. chopped fresh parsley
3 T. chopped fresh basil
1 t. salt; 2 t. black pepper
2 T. minced garlic
2 eggs (beaten)
4-5 c. Pepperidge Farm Herb Stuffing
2 blocks of Monterey Jack Cheese (sliced thickly)

Simply place all ingredients into a large enough bowl. With clean hands, (I prefer gloved hands) mix and blend all ingredients well. If needed add additional stuffing, if mixture not firm enough. In two loaf pans layer half the mixture on the bottom, sandwich sliced cheese on the bottom layer and cover then add additional mixture on top and seal the sides. Place loaf pan in a water bath (2 inches of water in pan large enough to place the pan of meatloaf in), cover with foil, bake at 450 for 1-1/2 hours until temperature in the middle reaches 170 degrees.

FREEDOM CAFÉ CHICKEN & SAUSAGE JAMBALAYA

3 lbs. Andouille, Chorizo, or spicy smoked sausage, sliced
2 quarts of chicken stock (store brought or homemade)
3 cups chopped onions
3 cups chopped green peppers
2 cup sliced celery
6 cans stewed tomatoes
5 T. chopped fresh basil
5 T. chopped fresh parsley
1/2 cup minced garlic
3 T. dry thyme
3 T. dry basil
3 T. dry oregano
1 T. cayenne pepper
½ cup Worcestershire sauce
4 T. onion powder
4 T. garlic powder
½ cup Creole seasoning (Zataran's)
½ cup of red wine
½ cup oil

Place oil in bottom of pot, sauté onions, peppers, celery until tender; add sausages and garlic; cooking until sausages are lightly browned; add chicken broth, tomatoes and the rest of the ingredients to the pot. Bring to a boil and then reduce to medium heat; cooking for 1 to 2 hours until everything is married. Serve over rice. It is better the next day.

STUFFED CHICKEN BREAST W/ GINGER ORANGE SAUCE

4 to 6 large boneless chicken breasts

Season chicken breast with poultry seasoning, garlic & onion powder, Lawry's seasoning salt; with a sharp knife make a slit in the thick side of the chicken breast; set aside in refrigerator

Stuffing:
1 small bunch of fresh spinach (chopped)
½ cup chopped onions
2 Tb minced garlic
2 Tb each of fresh chopped basil and parsley
1 cup of shredded Fontina or Smoked Gouda or both
1 cup chicken broth
1 small box of Stovetop Stuffing (chicken)
1 small jar of apricot preserves
¼ cup of white wine
1 stick butter
2 Tb oil

In a skillet melt 4 tablespoons of butter and oil, add chopped onions, spinach and garlic, sautéed spinach until wilted; add 1 jar of apricot preserves, dissolve; add fresh herbs, one box of your favorite stuffing mix with 1 cup of chicken broth. Take skillet off heat and add the shredded cheese, stirring until melted into mixture.

Cool stuffing mix in the refrigerator until ready to stuff chicken breast, stuff with as much as you like; place in baking dish, add melted the rest of the butter and add the white wine to the bottom of pan; cover and bake at 400 degrees for 45 minutes to an hour; temperature reading 170 degrees; serve with sauce.

ORANGE GINGER SAUCE

2 cans of frozen orange, pineapple, mango juice
2 bottles of Iron Chef Orange Glaze with Ginger
1 T. of fresh grated fresh ginger
2 T. minced garlic
2 T. Worcestershire sauce

In a small heavy gauge sauce pan mix all of the ingredients together; stirring constantly; adjust seasoning according to your taste. Serve over stuffed chicken breast.

Note: I find the Iron Chef Glaze at Hannaford's Grocery Store; if you can't find it use 2 jars of orange marmalade with 2 T. of grated fresh ginger.

JERK SAUCE

4 Scotch Bonnet Peppers
1 large onion grated
5 T. garlic minced
1 bunches scallions, chopped
1 T. Basil, Thyme, oregano (mixed)
2 T. Cinnamon
2 T. Allspice
1 cup Worcestershire sauce
½ cup vegetable oil
1 cup apple cider vinegar
2 T. salt
2 T. Black pepper
1 cup brown sugar
½ cup dark Rum
2 cups orange juice
2 T. crushed Habanera peppers
2 T. Chili Peppers
3 T. each of garlic, onion powder
4 T. grated fresh ginger
Zest of 2 lemons
Juice of 2 fresh lemons

Mix all of the above ingredients an airtight container.
Use half to marinate your chicken and reduce the
rest for sauce. This can be used also on spare ribs to
marinate and grill or slow cook in your oven or
cooker. The longer you marinade your meats the

better the flavor; so always marinade at least overnight.

JAMES' SWEET TEA & LEMONADE

Everyone loved the sweet tea and lemonade at Freedom Café. These were the only two things I had nothing to do with — they were James' creation.

FREEDOM CAFÉ'S SWEET TEA

Lipton Regular Tea 10 to 16 Tea Bags (depends on how strong you want it)
1 gallon of water
2 cups of sugar

Place tea bags in a pot filled with a gallon of water and bring to a rolling boil for a minute or two; then turn off the heat and let it stand for ten minutes and remove the bags from the water. Add approximately 2 cups of sugar or more, sweeten to taste. Stir until sugar is dissolved in the warm tea, chill or pour over ice and enjoy.

FREEDOM CAFÉ'S LEMONADE

Real Lemon Juice from concentrate
4 cups of water
¾ cup of Real Lemon juice
¾ cup of sugar

Combine ingredients and stir until sugar is dissolved. Serve over ice. Adjust taste accordingly (lemonade/sugar). Enjoy!

Chapter Four: Back to Mississippi

After 35 years of being away from home I am returning to the actual home in which I was raised. James and I are returning to Edwards, Mississippi to the same land and the same home, with renovations over the years, that I described in this chapter. Yes, you can go home again, particularly if God directs you too!

I was born October 8, 1956 in Washington, D.C. After a series of bad babysitters, my mother decided it was time to leave Washington, D.C. and return home to Edwards, Mississippi. She also had another reason for wanting to return to Mississippi -- her mother's failing health. On April 25, 1958 she resigned her job at the Naval Gun Factory's Purchasing Department, simply stating her reason for leaving as "to stay at home." Soon afterward she was back in Mississippi with her five children in tow: Carolyn Elizabeth,

Marilyn Annette, Eunice Yvette, Janice Rozett, and only one son at that time, Robert Junior.

In leaving Washington, she left our father behind for what she thought was for good. When she arrived in Edwards she took money she had saved in Washington and contracted to have a house built right next door to her mother, Eunice. In the meantime, we lived with Grandma Eunice while the house was being built. The house was built on land that was just a few yards from old highway 80. It was a very busy highway and not exactly the safest place for five children and, eventually, six when my brother David was born in 1962. The good thing was that behind the house was nearly three acres providing lots of room for the family garden and a playground for us children.

The house that mom had built was square with fake brick siding. It had four bedrooms, a large living room with a huge picture window, a T-shaped hall that led directly to bedrooms - right to the bathroom and left to the dining room and kitchen. She eventually built a front porch, added another bedroom, and patio on the side. The patio and the yards were filled with brightly colored Zinnias, Four-a-Clocks, Candelabra trees, and huge Elephant Ears. Mom always had exotic and strange flowers in her yards. There were old red wagons filled with cactus and car tires overflowing with flowers.

In the summer her flowers grew tall enough to be seen at the bottom of the picture window. It looked like a framed picture. The living room was off limits to us children and reserved for company only. There were hardwood floors and a gas heater that resembled a fireplace with two granite shaped logs on each side and the flame in the middle. Although it changed over the years, the first few years mom had a 50's white vinyl couch and chair. There was a vintage looking large framed picture of a winding country tree-lined road with mountains with light reflecting through them. The room was painted light pastel blue, filled curio cabinets with lots of porcelain figurines and an old red bookshelf filled with books marked the room.

Next to the living room was the dining room, which housed a huge wooden table that could accommodate the eight of us at meal times. The kitchen was next to the dining room, divided only by the semi-round kitchen counter built right in the middle; it served as mom's cooking counter, and the place where she lined up the food, sometimes buffet-style. Mom loved pastel colors and it showed in the kitchen. One wall where the kitchen sink was situated was painted a pastel pink. On the adjacent wall, the stove was painted a light green. Right above the sink, a huge window with sheer white curtains allowed her to look out at the land next door while she washed dishes. Above the stove was a homemade white shelf decorated with colorful knitted potholders, old-fashioned eggbeaters and cooking utensils hanging on hooks. The kitchen was my favorite room. I loved eating and helping momma cook. There's a snapshot of me when I was around three standing in front of the kitchen counter with my hands over my head, smiling as I waited to eat. In the background you can see the counter laden with a coconut cake, roast, fruit bowl, homemade biscuits and a goose. I'm sure it was Thanksgiving Day in 1959.

Behind the kitchen was the back porch which lead to what we called "down the hill" where our garden and playground were. The landscape was level where the house was built, immediately thereafter it began to slope downward into the valley where the garden was. Then it sloped upward again on a knoll where a very old cedar tree grew right on a knoll where the land leveled out again. Beyond the knoll was a thick and dense forest. Grandmother had about three acres of land; mostly filled with pecan trees she had planted when she first purchased the land years earlier. The pecan orchard helped to sustain the family. It was her fall business. When she died it helped supplement our income.

Every year just after school started, into early fall, it would be time to harvest pecans. My brother Robert and my sister Carolyn would climb each of those seven pecan trees, shaking the limbs; pecans rained down onto the ground. This was a family affair. We children stayed out of the range of the raining pecans until he had finished each tree. Then we would take our buckets, grocery bags, and tubs, and began picking them and filling our containers. Mom would load up the car with the pecans and drive to Vicksburg where she would sell them, earning money to help with school clothes for her children.

After the initial harvest whatever pecans remained mom allowed us to harvest and sell downtown at Miss Dolly's Country Store. The money we made from the sale we were allowed to keep for ourselves. Miss Dolly's store was housed in one of the oldest buildings downtown. The walls were old wooden planks that had never seen stain or paint, but had aged a deep dark brown. The store was long and wide with old-fashioned counters running down the sides of each wall. The room had one naked light bulb hanging in the center of the store. It looked like a barn. When you first walked into the store it took a few seconds before your eyes could adjust to the darkness. On the floor in front of the counters were large wooden barrels filled with loose soda crackers and vanilla wafers. Huge rounds of rich yellow cheddar cheese dotted the counter tops. This cheese was a favorite for the cotton-pickers who came into the store to buy lunch in the summer time; their lunch usually consisted of a can of sardines, a piece of cheese, crackers, vanilla wafers and a cold orange drink.

There was a scale in the middle of one of the counters where we would place our small bags of pecans to be weighed and sold for a few cents per pound. The dollar or two that we earned we almost immediately spent. During Christmas time we would buy those big peppermint sticks and lemons. We would break the peppermint sticks in half, stick them into the lemon and suck up the sour juice through the candy, which sweetened it.

Mom also saved some of the pecans from the harvest to make pecan pralines for us. She would give us pecans to crack and shell, "Make sure you keep the pecans halves whole without breaking the meat," she instructed us. "Yes, mom," we would respond eagerly as we waited to take those red bricks from the front yard and use them as nutcrackers; gently, we brought them down on those brown and black speckled pecan shells, being careful not to crush them too hard. After we had shelled enough pecans momma would inspect them and take out the bad halves.

Then she proceeded to make her famous pecan pralines, with me right next to the stove watching her. Of course, I was her helper. My job was to rub softened butter over the brown parchment paper that she had spread out on the counter for the hot candy mix. This kept the candy from sticking to the paper. Using her best turquoise Dutch oven, from her set of the same color, she placed butter, Carnation milk, and brown sugar into the pot, stirring it constantly with a wooden spoon so it would not burn. She stirred the candy mixture sticking her candy thermometer in until it reached the magic number, *238°*. She would also test for readiness by dropping a few drops in a cold cup of water to see if it would harden to the soft ball stage.

Mrs. Ann's Pecan Pralines

1 cup white sugar
1 t. salt
1 cup brown sugar
1 T. butter
1/2 cup half n half
1-1/2 cup pecan halves

This is my mother's pecan praline recipe. It is nuttier and the candy is harder. Measure out all of your ingredients before you begin. Cover a cookie sheet with aluminum foil and generously butter. Have a candy thermometer handy. I always use a wooden spoon to stir the candy.

Using a heavy gauged saucepan, add sugars and half-n-half on medium-heat or high if you have a heavy bottomed pan; stir ingredients until mixed well. Stir constantly until mix thickens and begins to bubble; place thermometer in mix until it reaches 238 degrees. Then pan off heat. Add butter, salt, and pecans, and stir well. Quickly scoop up candy using a tablespoon and place on greased waxed paper on a cookie sheet. Let harden, then enjoy. Makes about one dozen.

Chapter Five: I Didn't Take To the Woods

Many of you have heard me say I came to Maine to "live in the woods and write". I really wanted to be a hermit. My plan was to seek God, write, garden, feed a few chickens and live a quiet life. Well, that did not happen because it wasn't God's will and I wasn't ready to live in the woods. I think I would have gone stir crazy.

What I did do was find as many places in the woods that I could go and spend a few days. I spent many days on the beach in Saco at Bayview Villa Convent and took and introduced many women to retreats in the sacred walls of the old building, sitting on the veranda in rocking chairs watching the water; or rising early in the morning and meeting our Savior at sunrise on the beach.

During one February I took a group of young women there, we wrapped ourselves in coats, scarves, mittens and walked the beach in the freezing cold because we wanted to grow spiritually and intimately with Him. God met us there on that frozen beach and changed our lives. Unfortunately, the convent is now closed.

The next place we spent time was in cottages at the Boathouse in Brooklin, Maine, right on the water. It was a real Maine experience and was always spiritually awesome experience. The last time several of us went to the Boathouse, which actually is an old boathouse converted to a cottage, it sits over the water. It was a stormy night and we had carried wood down from the woodpile, and there was snow on the ground, but that didn't stop us. We settled into a night of wind blowing across the bay, the fireplace was roaring brightly as we sat wrapped in throws, hot beverages in hand, just fellowshipping and drinking in the moment. We still talk about that stormy winter's night on the water front.

Then through my dear friends, Don and Cindy Rowe, I was given a key to their cabin in the woods to use whenever I wanted to escape and relax. It is really not a cabin more a lodge, but it is in the midst of a cathedral of trees on a wooded hill. There is a brook that runs through the property providing that ever comforting sound of running water. I would sit on the deck at night and listen to the brook and look up at the amazing night sky – it was a breath of fresh air to weary souls.

That's the place where James and I went to really be alone and to do some real soul searching and writing. What great friends, they provided me my opportunity to escape to the woods when I really needed a break. Thanks guys.

While it is true that I never really took to the woods of Maine, I was able escape to them quite a bit nonetheless.

Chapter Six: Conversations

I have had a myriad of conversations with customers and friends at Freedom Café. While I cannot list them all there have been a few recent ones that are worth sharing.

Just the other day while waiting in my doctor's office, as usual, being among an elderly white population, I was the only black, dread-locked person in the room, which is not unusual for me. There was an older Mainer with a thick Maine accent, he had on jeans, boots and a plaid suit, and he appeared to be in his early seventies. He was chatting it up with the locals there that he knew and I was reading the forms I needed to fill out to get my medical records sent to Mississippi. As I sat there, after the gentleman he was talking to left after offering him a ride, of which he declined because someone was coming to pick him up and later take him to the grocery store; he turned to me and said "How do like this winter", I replied "I love it, no snow", he laughed and then he said "I like your shoes," I responded, "Thanks, they are very comfortable", he said, "did you get them at Wal-Mart", I said no, I got them at a little store downtown." "Nice he said." Just then his ride came; he got up, picked up his bag, said, "Have a good day", "you too, I replied, and then slowly got up and moved toward the door, and left. I couldn't help but smile at the pleasant exchange between us.

Again, it reminded me that I have lived here in Maine among a different people and a different culture, but this old man reminded me of something more important – we are all the same – souls – human beings living and trying to share a world. The best thing we can do is not to judge people by outward appearances, or how they talk, or what they look like; because this man had a gentle soul. There have been many times when I have judged and been judged, but one important lesson that God has been quick to remind me of is "man judges from the outward appearance but God judges from the heart – the inward man," the part that we humans cannot "see". In that few minutes in the doctor's office that scripture was, again, a lesson in real life.

_____

One day a man came into the café, large heavy-set white man from the South, Florida I believe. I seated him and as usual, started a conversation as this was his first time at the café. He told me he had heard great things about the food and wanted to see if it was really southern. I replied, okay, you are the judge. I took his order and brought him his meal. He began to eat, and I continued to take care of other customers, when I returned to his table he had only good things to say about the food. At the end of his meal, I sat down and asked him how did he come to Maine?

We talked about the fact that, in all likelihood, in the South we would not be sitting at the same table and having this deeply personal conversation – a white man that admitted he used to be racist until he became a Christian; and a black woman who sat and listened to him share his heartbreaking life story. He grew up tough but made a business for himself in construction; his partner took him for all he had in a lawsuit; he had lost everything that he had worked for. He and his wife had come to Maine because their daughter lived here and they wanted to see and help with the grandkids. He was praying to see what God wanted them to do. Meanwhile, he was trying to heal and restore his life.

I encouraged him and we prayed together at the end of the meal; I gave him his meal for free and told him to bring his wife and daughter, and the grandkids he dearly loved; and he left.

This reminded me again, that souls have no color.

November 2, 2009,

Dear Janice, It was a pleasure meeting you and James at your Freedom Café; the food was delicious! Our new acquaintances and the conversation were added treats. Jimmy and I enjoyed reading your book. Thank you for sharing your story. I hope our paths cross again. Sincerely, Maxine S.

If you have ever been a minority in a place, you will appreciate this story. One Thursday night in October 2009, the café was unusually slow; in fact, we had no customers the first hour. In a matter of minutes four very distinguished African American customers came through the door, about five minutes apart. There was Maxine and her husband who were passing through on business; there was a Colby member of the board of trustees that I knew and who always come by when in town; and a professional actor and singer who was staging a one man show at Colby – all black. At first I was, WOW! What is this about, jokingly I told them I had not had this many African Americans in the café at one time in a long time. The six of us, James and myself included, sat down and talked about the state of blacks in this country; the headlines that troubled us;

the way it used to be when we worked in community; the need to rescue our children and our neighborhoods; and the black church; it was a small piece of who we are and a reminder that we can still sit and intelligently discuss the state of affairs. It was uplifting and informative as they were coming from all areas of the life and the country with different experiences, but the same cultural concerns. I enjoyed the meeting of the minds.

———————————

Along those lines, back in September 2008, a lovely, well dressed, very pleasant older white woman brought her family to the café for dinner. She lived in New Hampshire. After dinner when she came to the counter to pay and purchase my cookbook, we began a conversation. She told me that she was a descendent of slave traders.

In our conversation, I was engaged to see the irony of it all, that here I was a descendent of slaves and she a descendent of slave traders, having this conversation in a soul food café in Maine; free of the tension of race; just two souls having a discussion about a dark time in the history of this country. I told her that my mother had worked hard to teach us that all men were created equal by our Creator God; and that she was not to be blame for what her ancestors had done; though she still felt a tinge of guilt because she could see we still had a long way to go.

I agreed and said but look at us here, having this conversation, and talking from the heart about our history. She agreed. Later that year, during the Christmas season, she sent me a copy of her cousin's book "Inheriting the Trade" by Thomas Norman DeWolf. She wrote in her note with the book that her whole family was involved in the slave trade and that they were the "most prominent slave traders of their day." She continued, "It occurred to me that I should send you the book...you are a writer and I thought you might be interested." I had shared with her my mother's work and travels and my desire and work regarding the slave trade and the "peculiar institution" of slavery in this country.

I thanked her as it reminded me of part of my journey and destiny. I have written quite a bit of work on America and slavery and its effect on African Americans, Christianity and our society at large. I thanked her because she was only reminding me again of the work that I had started before coming to Maine; and the work I would now pick up again as I leave.

Chapter Seven: Mom's Legacy

My mother died in 1998, less than a year after I had moved to Maine. She too was a historian and writer of Ancient Black Biblical History. She had traveled throughout Africa many, many times, researching her work in Egypt's pyramids and the ancient tombs of the Pharaohs in Thebes, traversing the Nile and Ethiopia. Egypt and Ethiopia are very important in ancient biblical history and civilizations of mankind. My mother, a devout Christian, found her identity in Christ and in His Word, and she wanted to share this often overlooked and distorted history of African Americans and the world. She died before she could complete her book "Lost Horizons of Ancient Black History," yet unpublished. Her purpose and destiny was to help black people know their God and who He had created them to be, not just a history of slavery in America.

In 1991, I traveled with her once on an African American History tour to Ghana, Ivory Coast and Senegal. We visited the slave forts along the coast; and attended lectures on slave history at several of the universities.

At that time I was a student at the University of Kansas, School of Journalism. I began to research volumes of works on "Slave Narratives" from which I wrote several works, yet unpublished. In the meantime, I wrote an award winning play entitled "Sistahs & Brothers In Identity Crisis: African Americans in Search of Self"; I also spoke at many events on slave history and the need for racial understanding and reconciliation, and published a few articles on the subject. Then I moved to Maine in 1996, and put away my works as there were not many opportunities to use my work here.

Back to 1998, after my mother's funeral, we were going through some of her personal things and I grabbed a file folder with some of her writings. I brought it home and stuck it away for 12 years.

When God began directing us back to Mississippi, my immediate response was "this has something to do with my mom"; she prayed something because I knew I didn't want to return there.

I struggled with this feeling that this had something to do with "mom", even the fact that I would be returning to her home, walking through the same rooms that I grew up in, the same land that I played and worked on. I just didn't know what.

Then, on February 23, my best friend Norma Johnson died at the age of 68 having literally starved to death because of Alzheimer's and dementia. She basically stopped eating and because she was a nurse, had a living will. No heroics. I wasn't devastated because I knew she had her mind back and was no longer suffering. She was the first person that I had led to Christ back as a very new Christian in 1986. Even more important was the fact that she loved Maine and it was because of her that I came here in 1996, interviewed for the job, and eventually moved to Maine. She and I had come together to go on a spiritual retreat in Bar Harbor, Maine on that fateful trip in 1996.

Literally, Norma had been God's angel to lead me to the next leg of my journey which was Maine, now that I was moving out of Maine; she died just three months before I was to leave Maine. I knew her death was significant in the spiritual realm; first things happen in the natural realm before they manifest in the spiritual realm. Norma had been my best friend; she prayed for me more than anyone on the face of earth, after my mother. God used her to encourage me on my spiritual journey and to pursue my calling. She would call me and asked, "Jan, what's going on, God has been waking me up to pray for you almost every night?" And there was always some crisis or need during these times; mostly my sanity and health. Now, she was gone – what did this mean?

It was a sobering event; the two women that I knew prayed for me and were very important in my life journey were dead – my mother and my friend Norma. Both having died after I moved to Maine; I sensed God saying it was time for me to run toward my destiny.

The same night that Norma died, I felt God telling me to get out all my work on African American Slave History and get it ready to use; and as I was processing this work, He gave me a mandate to "Tell my people who they are?" Finally revealing to me that my mother had written the first part of the book on Ancient Black Biblical History, and I had written the second part on the African Diaspora and enslavement in America. My next assignment is to complete this work my mother began; a collaborative work between my mother and me. I had chills thinking about it, what a privilege and a God given legacy. She had been traveling and writing this history over 20 years ago in the 1980's; while I began my writing on slavery and its detrimental effects on black people as a student in the early 1990's.

As I gathered her articles and read them, I traveled with her to the pyramids of Egypt, to Thebes, and Ethiopia; neither of us realizing that the two works was destined to come together at the appointed time and place; which is NOW. I have picked up the baton and I am running with it. It is a privilege to complete my mother's work that God destined for us both. It was her life focus and her destiny to start and for me, her daughter, to finish.

Thanks for being a part of this project.

IN HIS LOVE,
Janice

Mississippi Addendum

The last three months before we closed we were packed – reservations completely full for three straight months. The phone continued to ring constantly ending with very disappointed people on the other end. There was no way we could squeeze any more people into that dining room.

It was busy and hectic, very bittersweet for James and I, knowing that we needed to close and move on but having put blood sweet and tears into that café and community in Waterville.

As I write this addendum, July 19, 2011, we have been in Mississippi for just over a year. We closed the restaurant on May 29, 2010 and packed up and left June 2, 2010, arriving in Mississippi June 4, 2010. The trip was just as traumatic as the first one in April when we drove the big U-Haul and moved out belongings.

On Memorial Day weekend all of our Freedom Café family came and spent hours cleaning, packing, loading, and some of us crying. The last Saturday night had been the first time I allowed myself to cry. Lori Dumont and arranged for the Gawlers, my favorite musical family of fiddlers to come in and surprise us. The café was packed when they came in and began singing with their beautiful smiles and melodic rhythmic music – I cried. That was it. The shell broke and the tears came flooding down my cheeks. It was then, in the midst of a café full of community friends and family, many of whom had brought us gifts of earrings and a small hand painted picture of a blueberry field which hangs in my office today, and all the "we'll miss you", "we love you" and "farewell good friends"; I knew I had been a part of something very special and it would be very much missed.

Now to the present, Mississippi is not Maine. Maine changed us in many ways and it didn't take long in hot and humid Mississippi to realize – Wow! I miss Maine. The fall here doesn't even compare with the beautiful changes in colors of Maine' falls; and I am landlocked and haven't seen the ocean since I arrived. I miss Maine – it was a retreat without having to leave the state.

My senses were jarred once we unpacked and settled into our family home. The first jarring was the 100 degree heat and the humidity so thick you could drink it. I literally thought I would die. It had been over 35 years since I had experienced a

Mississippi summer because I visited in the fall and winter.

Our first major investment was air conditioners. Phew! I spent the summer in the house, only venturing out on the deck in the mornings and evenings. It soon became evident that we were living among a bird paradise. Surrounded by old ancient trees, thick groves, the birds have their own sanctuary and James began to really enjoy watching and listening to the birds – all kinds – everywhere.

I began familiarizing myself with family and as is the reality of most of our families – that personalities indeed are different. But all in all, James and I are "different ducks" and quacking isn't always enjoyed. So the first year I began writing and researching the book of Ancient Black History that my mother began. It was too hot to even think about a garden so I spent lots of money on groceries – more than I spent in Maine.

Last summer I did a community play with the teenagers, another play for women in the Bible, and ministered at several women's meetings and programs at surrounding churches. In December we gave away all the dolls I had purchased at Mardens to the needy children; hosted a woman's study in my home; and worked as a minister at a local church.

Basically, I immersed myself into the community, writing a community newsletter and in the fall tried my hands at a small café in my sister's ice cream shop. That was indeed short-lived. The people enjoyed my cooking and the large portions – but this town is too small to support a café and I realized I didn't want to put my apron on again; food service for me was done.

So in March of this year God opened the door for me to get a position at the University of Mississippi Medical Center, in the office of Research and Scholarship as an administrative assistant using my writing/editing skills and learning and using more computer skills than I thought possible. I like the job because it pushes me to improve my own writing and work.

Many of you remember me calling Mississippi "the same ole south with a new dress on" and unfortunately I was right. When I went to work the dress came off and the real deal was exposed.

It is the plantation system – the only difference is they moved from the plantation to the service centers, hospitals, kitchens, schools, etc. Yes, there are blacks working in places that they never had the opportunity to do before. There are many educated blacks working in decent jobs. BUT the reality is most are not in power and their positions are always underneath the structure of this system.

It is as though they have declared a truce among themselves – you stay in your place and I in mine. Don't cross the lines – and definitely don't speak to me or think that I want to be friendly. It is so thick you can cut it with a knife – but the veneer of southern hospitality (now my southern hospitality in Maine was real), they grin and smile but it doesn't mean a thing. Then the blacks have accepted and acquiesced knowing exactly how to navigate the dangerous roadways in the "South". Basically, I hate it. It is two different nations and peoples sharing the same place but not the same space. And the black communities are just as fragmented, fractured and divided as ever.

I am so glad that I had lived up North in Maine. Yes, I know there are prejudice people in Maine, they are everywhere, but living in Maine meant I could breathe and move from place to place in peace; speak to people and people spoke back; and helped whenever you needed a hand; and were friendly though not pushy, for fifteen years. I made great friends in Maine, and people I will be in touch with for life.

It was having experienced this that gave me the background and experience to realize just how different Mississippi really is. If I had not met and lived among the people of Maine, which is 98% white, and had the freedom to open "Freedom Café" and be successful at it; and be allowed to become part of the fabric of a community where I was the minority for real, I would probably take a different attitude from my experiences here – but instead, I remember that not all people are the same regardless of the color of their skin – and you decide their character by their fruit.

Yes, I still miss Maine but Maine gave me what I needed to be able to move to Mississippi and become a part of the solution down here and not part of the problem. Thanks again Mainers!

FAREWELL FROM JAMES:

Thanks for having dinner with us, Jan and I have enjoyed sitting and talking with you at your table, getting to know you and you getting to know us. My journey has just begun. My Heavenly Father has taught me many things while living here in Maine. He has provided Freedom Café and Maine to be my training ground. In my autobiography "Testimony of James Swinton: A Search for Truth" at the end of my autobiography, "True Christianity: My Search Has Ended," you will find several conclusions God has helped me to come too. If you haven't read it, see our ministry website:

"breakingfreeministries.weebly.com."

Proceeds from the sale of this book will go to finishing and completing the work of my mother, Mrs. Anne Odene Smith; and to help spread the healing power of the gospel of Jesus Christ and to promote the healing of souls.

Other books by Janice Swinton: "Fleshly Adams: The Root & Fruit of Sexual Perversity"

Our web address is:

www.breakingfreeministries.weebly.com

Mailing Address:

P. O. Box 352; Edwards, Mississippi 39066

Thanks.

Made in the USA
Las Vegas, NV
21 December 2021